LOSE THE WAIT AND FEEL GREAT!

LOSE THE WAIT AND FEEL GREAT!

How to shed pounds of procrastination and find your true purpose.

Staci J. Scott, MHS

Disclaimer

This book is designed to provide information and motivation to the reader. It is provided with the understanding that the author and/or publisher is not engaged to render any type of psychological, legal, or any other kind of professional advice. The content found within is the sole expression and opinion of its author. No warranties or guarantees are expressed or implied by the author's and/or publisher's choice to include any of the content in this volume. Neither the publisher nor the author shall be liable for any physical, psychological, emotional, financial, or commercial damages, including, but not limited to, special, incidental, consequential or other damages.

1st edition, March 2021

ISBN: 978-0-578-80559-7

Printed in the United States of America

DEDICATION

To my daughter, Rienne Scott, who motivates and inspires me every day. Through her words and actions, she encourages me to boldly present to the world my true and authentic self without apologies or fear.

To women everywhere who have sacrificed their own slice of happiness, their dreams, plans, and desires – this is for you; for us. Our wait is over.

CONTENTS

INTRODUCTION

I KNOW YOU'VE GOT A lot on your plate. Life can throw so many things at us that it's easy to become weighed down with what we have to do and spend less and less time focusing on what it is we're meant to do. We end up putting our hopes and dreams on the back burner and convincing ourselves that if we WAIT long enough one day, we'll find the time to get back to them. I know your to-do list is long. But believe me, this book is not another something to do or something to get through. This book is your very own personal trainer. If you let it, in only minutes a day, this book will help you shed your excess WAIT and get you moving toward your purpose and your passion.

How many times have you said, "I've always wanted to (fill in the blank)"? Your goal could be to write a book, travel overseas, reconnect with an old friend, lose weight, find true love, or start a business. Oh, wait a minute; those are things I've said! And this isn't about me. Or is it? Every writer writes from a personal space deep within themselves, a space where their unique story unfolds. For me, so much of my adult life has centered on losing physical weight, but I'll talk more about that later. Right now, I want to focus on WAITING. Most of us have many hopes, dreams, goals, and aspirations. Some of us find it easy to stay the course and see all those wonderful ideas through to fruition. I applaud those folks. But I've been wondering what makes them different.

What drives them? And why is it that some of us, as well intending as we may be, why are some of us stuck? And, yes, I use the word "us" because when I began writing this manuscript, I was feeling stuck myself. People who know me might be surprised by that revelation. By all outward appearances I had a "good" job, was always on the go, and referred to by some as quite the social butterfly. Guess what? It was all a sham! The job I had back then was not one that I loved or was particularly passionate about – but it paid the bills. I was unhappy and knew it. But I couldn't seem to move beyond wanting something better. What was I waiting for? Turns out I was just waiting for ME to show up. So, Thursday, March 20th, 2014 at 11:55 p.m. I started writing. Ok – confession time. As you already know, the year is now 2021.

As you can imagine it's been quite a journey. After all it did take me 7 years to complete this book. Funny thing is, I've had this idea in my head for a while; the idea that procrastination is slowly killing me – killing us. And I wanted to play off the words wait and weight. As someone who used to tip the scales at nearly 300 pounds, weight is always on my mind. The result? I just decided to stop procrastinating and start writing. I wish I could say that I had this great aha moment, an epiphany, a moment of clarity, or at the very least some monumental life altering episode to get me writing again (notice I said again – I'll talk about that later in the book also). But I didn't. I simply made up my mind to start writing.

And that's the true point of this book – to get out of our own way and simply get STARTED. So, let's start this journey together. Let's talk, laugh, cry, explore –

but let's START. I promise you'll enjoy the ride.

By the way, this book is dedicated to my beautiful, intelligent, and gifted daughter Rienne. And, yes, I'm completely biased – what can I say I'm her mother! Rienne is my shero and the inspiration for this book. In 2013 Rienne was not happy with her life. At 27 years young this college graduate found herself living back at home and working a dead-end job. On a whim she applied for a teaching fellowship in another state. She was accepted. She moved to Baltimore and 3 months later was teaching high school English to 10th graders. She has a great apartment, excellent salary (of course teachers should be paid more), but most importantly she's much happier with her life. Rienne completely changed her life all because she stopped WAITING for things to get better. She decided in her mind that SHE could make things better – and she did. If she can do it so can we.

Now do you get it? Lose the WAIT and feel great! Let's get started…

I. BEGINNING YOUR WAIT LOSS JOURNEY

EVERY GREAT JOURNEY BEGINS WITH preparation. Whether it's a family vacation, educational goal, or even something as simple as what to do this weekend, planning is essential. We spend hours considering the implications, i.e., financial (Do I have enough money? Any money?"), physical (Is this a staycation or I am going somewhere?), familial (Who's going with me? The kids? Husband/wife? Just the girls/guys?), secular (Can I get the time off from work?), and psychological (Do I really want to go? I could just stay at home and binge watch Breaking Bad.)

Our Wait Loss journey requires advanced mental preparation too. First, we need to determine if we are ready to begin this journey. Your attitude toward your Wait Loss will significantly impact whether you will succeed. Take the quiz on the following pages and determine if you need to make any adjustments in your thought and behavior patterns before beginning your journey. Be honest with yourself and reply to each statement with a T for true if you agree and F for false if the statement does not apply to you.

WAIT LOSS READINESS QUIZ[1]

1. I have given much thought to my life and can pinpoint what I need to change. _____

2. I have accepted that I need to make permanent, not temporary, changes in my life in order to be successful. _____

3. I will only feel successful if I lose a lot of wait. _____

4. I have accepted the idea that it's best if I lose wait slowly. _____

5. I'm thinking of losing wait now because it's the right time for me, not because someone else thinks I should do it. _____

6. I think losing wait will solve other problems in my life. _____

7. I will only be successful if I have no "slip ups". _____

8. I am ready to commit time and effort every day to organizing my life and planning my Wait Loss activities. _____

9. Once I lose some initial wait, I may lose the motivation to keep going until I reach my ultimate goal. _____

10. I want to start a Wait Loss program even though my life is very stressful right now. _____
11. I'm not sure about this "Wait Loss" concept, but I'm willing to give it a try. _____

Scoring the WAIT LOSS READINESS QUIZ

To score the quiz, take a look at your answers to items 1,2,4,5,7,9. Score "1" if you answered "true" and "0" if you answered false. For items 3,6,8,10,11 score "0" for each true answer and "1" for each false answer. To get your total score, add the scores for all answers. Once you've totaled your scores – **throw them in the trash!**

This is not THAT kind of book. Let's take a quick water break. **(Throughout this book we'll pause for some hydration – interesting tips, facts, and suggestions to keep you moving forward and to keep your brain functioning properly.)**

Do you know why quizzes were put in women's magazines over 50 years ago? Turns out quizzes allowed the editors to reduce advice columns and give us ladies a chance to find out something we're always dying to know - how we measure up. Are we good mothers? Wives? Friends? Are we pretty enough? Are we kind? Loving? Sexy? Etc., etc. Those early quizzes assumed that we believed that we are flawed but somehow fixable by the magazine articles and pages. Pages that contain products being sold by their advertisers. It was a Jedi mind trick to get us to spend money. Those quizzes were designed to capitalize on our insecurities. And we bought it! Literally. Hook, line, and sinker!

But what about today? We know better right? Maybe. For the most part, quizzes have moved from the pages of magazines to the Internet. And yes, we are still obsessed with them. I'm guilty too. They can be cute and funny. They ask questions like what ice cream flavor are you or if you were a candy bar which one would you be. Who wouldn't want to know that? The truth is, we love quizzes because we're still desperate to know who we are, where we stand in the world, and how we compare to others. And we're secretly hoping we're better than other quiz takers.

Why is it we never ask WHO created the quiz? Who are these mystical beings who determined that my ice cream flavor match is mint? Mint?? Seriously?

Apparently, I am cool under pressure, calm, and collected at all times. I never shy away from a challenge. I thrive in stressful situations and my attitude is refreshing. OK – that does sound like me. But that's not the point. I decided to take the quiz again. This time I changed 2 answers, just 2, and suddenly my ice cream flavor match was chocolate. Now that's more like it! With those 2 small changes instantly, I became someone who cared deeply about those around me. Now, I lead with my heart in all that I do. People describe me as passionate. I'm a romantic but far from hopeless. Yeah, yeah, yeah. I'm flattered and it does sound like me. While those things were nice to read, we all know that if I took that quiz again and changed 3 answers my entire personality profile would change – again.

Here's the thing, I don't need a quiz to tell me what type of person I am, and YOU don't need a quiz to tell you when it's time to begin your Wait Loss journey. Just like me, you already know. Let's get back to it.

I want you to begin thinking about your perception of this concept of Wait Loss. Regardless of what I could tell about the meaning of your scores, only you will know when you are ready to begin. Go back to the beginning of the quiz. Notice I said, **"Take the quiz below and determine if you need to make any adjustments in your thought and behavior patterns before beginning your journey."** YOU make the ultimate determination - not me. And I happen to think that if you're holding this book in your hand, you're ready. So, here's the first lesson of Wait Loss: **Don't let anyone (including an author you've never met) dissuade you from pursuing your dream, your goal, or your vision.** Think about this.

What if I told you that your scores revealed that you weren't ready to begin your Wait Loss journey? What would you do? Would you stop? Would you agree with me? And if the answer to any of those questions is yes, then my next question would be - "why"? Only you can answer that. But remember too often in life we let other people tell us what to think, how to feel, what to do, or what not to do, and when to act. I say it's time for a change.

WAIT LOSS ACTIVITY #1

Go to a quiet place. Close your eyes. Breathe deeply for at least one full minute and try to quiet your mind. Don't think about the mortgage, the kids, the bills, the job, the leaky faucet, whether you remembered to take out the trash or walk the dog. At the end of the minute (or longer if you need it) complete the sentence (out loud), "I've always wanted to (fill in the blank)." And voila, you're ready!

Note – It should be said here that we must be realistic. Let's say a fifty-four-year-old man, who is approximately five feet four inches tall, with absolutely no skill for basketball always wanted to play the center position for the Philadelphia Seventy-Sixers basketball team. Chances are that dream is not going to come true. However, maybe that same man could volunteer at a youth program encouraging other (more athletically endowed) youngsters to pursue basketball. Maybe that same man could volunteer at the sports arena or learn what qualifications are needed to work for the Philadelphia 76ers franchise and begin obtaining those qualifications which would allow him to eventually apply for employment with the team. Get the point? It's ok to dream and dream big but at some point, you have to wake up and do the work as Iyanla Vanzant might say. In this case, doing the work involves understanding, embracing, and accepting our boundaries.

Notice I used the word boundaries and not limitations. The word limitation feels like a negative word to me so I'm going to avoid it. But the word boundary invokes a sense of knowing the realm that we can comfortably navigate. This also includes knowing ourselves, our strengths, likes, and dislikes. These aspects of our personality will help shape the scope of our personal universe. For me, I know that I love to do three things: help others, teach, and write. I am my happiest when I am doing one or more of those three things. Now, it's your turn. How will you define your personal universe?

Let's first start with understanding the concept. Consider the world around you. There is a school of thought that says that your world or universe is the result of something you created, a response to your every thought, word, and action. Think about that for a minute. You create your personal universe. YOU! Not anyone or anything around you. Just YOU. Do you realize how powerful you are? Now take a look at your personal universe. No matter what you may think about it; it's great, wonderful, so-so, not that good – you have made it what it is, and you have the power to change it. You are the master, and you are in control. Not convinced yet? Try this exercise: Imagine you are biting into a lemon. What does it taste like? What do you remember about lemons? Are you making a face right now? Are you frowning as you remember the bitter taste?

What we know is that there is no actual lemon. You are responding to a mental image you've created in your mind. Remember your mind is a powerful tool. What you believe, think, feel, imagine, act upon, and speak all contribute to your personal universe. So why not try believing the best about yourself and your dreams? Why not try thinking that it's possible for those dreams to come true? Why not try feeling the immeasurable joy, anticipation, and excitement of success? Why not try imagining what your life will be like, what YOU will be like as you begin to work toward those dreams? Why not try acting upon some of these suggestions and speaking your desires into existence? WHY NOT? What's the worst that could happen? Even if I'm totally wrong you won't be any worse off. You'll be right where you started, albeit a bit more miserable.

And who needs/wants that? But what if I'm right? Imagine being happy about your choices and where you are in your life. Imagine the possibilities. Too often we limit ourselves by imagining that our possibilities are impossible.

Consider this quote by Muhammad Ali:

"Impossible is just a big word thrown around by small men who find it easier to live in the world they've been given, than to explore the power they have to change it. Impossible is NOT a fact. It's an opinion. Impossible is NOT a declaration. It's a dare. Impossible is potential. Impossible is temporary. Impossible is nothing."

Time for another water break:

Cassius Clay, before he became Muhammad Ali, was a 22-year-old Olympic gold medalist when he won his first heavyweight championship. When he refused to serve in the military and participate in the Vietnamese war, Muhammad Ali was convicted of draft evasion, sentenced to 5 years in prison, banned from boxing and stripped of his title. Faced with these obstacles many thought his boxing career was over. No doubt some encouraged Ali to do something else; find another career.

During his ban from boxing, he supported his family via paid speaking engagements. He was good at it. We all know how charismatic he was. Why did he not give up on boxing? Because boxing was both his passion and his purpose.

He never stopped believing in his dream to become the greatest of all time. No way was that dream impossible for him. Was it deferred a bit? Yes. Did he have to overcome serious obstacles? Yes. But he knew in his heart that "**nothing is impossible and impossible is nothing**".

Let's take a moment to pause and breathe through that last sentence. Take a deep breath and say: Nothing is impossible. Impossible is nothing. Again – deep breath and say: Nothing is impossible. Impossible is nothing. Repeat these steps each time you begin to doubt your ability to accomplish your dreams and fulfill your life's *purpose.*

When people tell you that your dream is impossible, remember YOU have the power to create and shape your personal universe. You do not have to accept the world as it is. Impossible is nothing and nothing is impossible! Each of us are created with mind-blowing talents, gifts and abilities that too often lay dormant within us because we are too busy acting out the roles given to us by life. We are mothers, cooks, chauffeurs, fathers, caregivers, maids, nurses, teachers, comforters, housekeepers, bankers, maids, etc., etc.

And yes, chances are we can't just give up those roles and honestly, we don't really want to give them up. But at some point, in our lives we allowed those roles to consume our entire world or universe.

WAIT LOSS ACTIVITY #2

Close your eyes and see yourself in the middle of your universe. It may feel as if you are in the eye of your very own tornado and that's ok. Life is sometimes stormy. But as you're standing there with the wind blowing, your kids crying, bill collectors calling, and dinner burning remember you have a purpose. Whisper to the wind, to your higher power, and to yourself - **I can do it. I will do it starting today.** You don't have to shout out loud or make a lot of noise to be heard or to make an impact. Whispering can sometimes have a greater impact that shouting because it forces us to pay close attention to what's being said.

My goal is that upon completion of this book you will begin to value your voice above all others that attempt to vie for your attention and distract you from your goals, your dreams, and your purpose. My hope is that you find the courage to trust and follow your voice and let it guide you to greater fulfillment in your life's journey. And by the way, I hope those things for me too!

II. SOME THINGS ARE REALLY NOT WORTH THE WAIT

SOMEWHERE ALONG THE WAY CHRONIC procrastinators including me bought into the message that anything worth having is worth waiting for. Don't rush things. It will come to you. Let the universe bring it to you. Jack London once said, "If a thing is worth doing, it is worth doing well. **If it is worth having, it is worth waiting for**. If it is worth attaining, it is worth fighting for. If it is worth experiencing, it is worth putting aside time for."

On the one hand he's saying it's ok to wait for a thing, but if that thing happens to be worth experiencing then we should put aside time for it. Huh?? Did he mean put aside time to pursue it or to wait for it? In either case, I think Jack got it wrong. I think anything worth having should be worth our effort to obtain it. Therefore, it seems to me that we must believe in the worth of the thing to be obtained, i.e., the goal, dream, or desire. And before we can believe in the worth of the thing to be obtained, we must first believe in the worth of the originator of the goal, dream or desire.

We must believe that we are intelligent, acceptable, worthy, capable, resilient, unstoppable, and undeniable! And so of course we've suddenly come up with a great idea, and of course we're going to pursue it! Why not? Why WAIT? Why indeed?

AHA Moment (Personal Experience)

In the interest of transparency and personal integrity I need to admit something to you. As I said in the introduction, I began writing this book on March 20, 2014. I started seriously working on the book again on March 13, 2019 – YIKES! So, I was forced to ask myself what took me so long? Why did I put off writing every day? I had all these ideas in my head around procrastination and helping people get unstuck and here I was stuck. It took me a while to understand what was going on with me. I didn't believe in my worth enough to believe that someone would want to read my words, let alone actually act because of them.

One day a very good friend noticed a trend with me. I asked Kimberly to read the first two chapters of this book. I wanted to get her feedback, her thoughts on the content thus far. She gave me several great suggestions but there was one comment that hit me like a ton of bricks. She noticed that I used a lot of citations and references.

In the draft that she read (remember just the first two chapters) there were at least 10 citations and quotes. In my mind, I was falling back on my grad school days and faithfully citing my sources.

My wonderfully astute friend asked me why I felt the need to rely on so many other people's opinions. She told me to trust my own voice. Wow! That was an AHA moment for me. Was that my issue? Did I not trust my voice or value my own opinion? I began thinking about my daily life.

I am a big fan of quotes. I can find a quote to fit almost any situation. I use them at work in emails, memos, etc. With Google's help I can find quotes from celebrities, scholars, politicians, athletes, etc. You'll see them throughout this book. In my personal life, I send cards and write letters to friends and family members. Again, I include quotes, poems, and even scriptures – could it be because I didn't believe that my thoughts were enough? Credible? Worthy?

Once upon a time I felt unworthy, unbelievable and even insufficient. I felt that I was not enough. It wasn't until I embarked on my own Wait Loss journey that I began to believe the message I plan to share with you. I know what's it like to experience these feelings and sometimes they come back. And that's ok. Because I know that about myself it's something I work on constantly.

Once I realized the possibility of its reemergence, I was able to move forward with a clear plan of action. Remember what I said in Chapter 1:

> *My goal is that upon completion of this book you will value your voice above all others that attempt to vie for your attention and distract you from your goals, your dreams, and your purpose. My hope is that you find the courage to trust and follow your voice and let it guide you to greater fulfillment in your life's journey.*

By forging ahead and writing this book I am finding MY courage to trust and follow MY voice as it leads ME to greater fulfillment in my life's journey. This is a journey we will take together.

Lesson: As you embark upon your Wait Loss journey don't be afraid to have a heart-to-heart talk with someone you love and trust. Talk to them about your desire to fully embrace your dreams and goals. Ask them what they think could be holding you back. You just might have an AHA moment of your own.

Let's get back to the idea of Wait Loss. Much has been written on why people procrastinate or put off pursuing their dreams. I think most of us can agree that the number one reason is **FEAR**. FEAR that it won't work, that we'll fail, that people will laugh, that it won't make any money, that no one will support the idea, that people will think it's stupid, that people will think I'm stupid, that people won't get it, that it will take much longer than I thought, that I'm not as smart as I think I am, that I'm not smart at all, that my kids will laugh at me, that I won't make my (kids, husband, wife, mother, father, sister, brother, grandparents, teachers, etc.) proud of me, that I'll let everyone down, that I'll let myself down. And the list goes on.

Wow! That's a lot of pressure to put on ourselves. Just WHO are these "people" and why do they exert so much control over our lives and thoughts?

> *Consider Dr. Daniel Amen's 18/40/60 rule:*
>
> *When you're 18 you worry about what everybody is thinking about you; When you're 40, you don't care what anybody thinks of you.*
>
> *When you're 60 you realize nobody's been thinking about you at all!*

No matter where you fall in that timeline eventually you will come to the realization that YOUR voice, YOUR opinion, and YOUR truth is what matters most.

II. Some Things Are Really NOT Worth the Wait

I saw a post recently that said what other people think of you is none of your business. I love that!! We spend so much time obsessing over the opinion of people who ultimately don't matter. Why?

Because we seek approval. We want to be liked, loved, respected, and well thought of. There's nothing wrong with wanting those things. The danger comes in allowing those thoughts to consume us. Like, love and respect yourself first. Think highly of yourself. Don't wait until you're 40 years old or older to accept yourself as you are. Don't wait for the results of a quiz to remind you of your inner superpower – awesomeness. And please do not wait until you are 60 years old to recognize what is true at this very moment. ***Right now, you have everything you need to walk in and live the life you've always imagined for yourself.***

WAIT LOSS ACTIVITY #3

Take a deep breath. Repeat this affirmation:

I am intelligent, acceptable, worthy, capable, resilient, unstoppable, and undeniable! I am a force to be reckoned with! I can do this! I will do this! I am amazing!

I must tell you, I never thought of myself as an affirmation saying type of person. But this stuff works! Try it. Say it as often as you need to until you begin to believe it, until the words are as natural as your name. Write it on notes and post it around your house, your office, your car – everywhere! Try it.

Speaking of posting things around your house. Do you remember the tv show Being Mary Jane? It starred Gabrielle Union. She played the role of Mary Jane Paul, a highly successful news anchor who lived in a gorgeous home, wore nothing but designer clothes and shoes, drove a nice car and was super ambitious.

Despite all of these things something was always missing in life. As she tried to make sense of her life and find her true purpose, she chose to use quotes as affirmations and sources of inspiration. If you're struggling to come up with affirmations of your own remember it's ok to use the quotes of others to kick start your inspiration. Feel free to use the quotes in this book. They worked for me.

Reject Negative Thoughts

It's not enough to repeat positive thoughts. As chronic procrastinators we need to retrain our brains to think positively, to rid ourselves of our "automatic negative thoughts". What are these thoughts? Simply put, they are negatively framed interpretations of what we think is happening to us. Here are some common examples:

1. Always/Never Thinking - Thinking in words like always, never, no one, everyone, every time, everything.

   a. **Example: No one will like or buy my cupcakes.**

2. Focusing on the negative – seeing only the bad in a situation.

   a. **Example – You invite 50 people to your open house and only 40 show up. You stress out over the 10 who didn't make it.**

3. Predicting the worst possible outcome to a situation.

   a. **Example: When I make my sales pitch, the audience will think that I don't really know what I'm talking about.**

4. Mind Reading - Believing that you know what others are thinking, even though they haven't told you.

   a. **Example: (thoughts) My boss didn't speak to me. She's mad at me; doesn't like me.**

5. Thinking with your feelings – believing negative feelings without ever questioning them.

   a. **Example: You start sentences with "I feel". I feel like a failure. I feel like you don't love me. I feel like everyone is against me.**

6. Thinking in words like should, must, ought, or have to.

   a. **Example: I ought to spend more time writing my book. I should spend more time with my kids.**

If we're not careful that little voice in our head can become the disc jockey of our lives, replaying those same negative tunes over and over again. It's time to change the station! Time to get rid of those pesky **Automatic Negative Thoughts:**

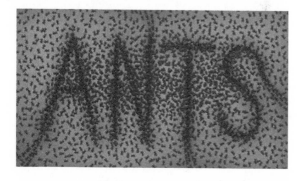

Here are a few tricks to help train your brain to get rid of these annoying traits.

1. The first step is to recognize and pay close attention to these thoughts when they pop into your brain – be prepared for them. Acknowledge them and tell yourself that it's just a thought and thoughts aren't facts. Recognize them for what they are; petty annoyances that have no real meaning. Speak the thought out loud (or in your head if you're not alone), examine it and reframe it. Example: The funders will never listen to me. This is an Always Never Thinking ANT. Crush it by saying instead: The funders are fair and impartial businesspersons. They will give me a chance to present my ideas and provide honest feedback for moving forward.

2. The second step is to challenge it. How would you respond if someone were to start saying negative things about you that you knew weren't true? Would you simply accept it and become defeated? Probably not. The same way you would challenge that person – challenge yourself and that negative thought. Don't let it defeat you.

3. Step three is to replace the negative thought with a positive one. Example: Instead of saying, "I'm going to mess up this speech" say

"My speech will be amazing and will touch someone's life today."

Remember: Recognize the negative thought, challenge it, and replace it with something positive. Make this a habit and eventually the negative thoughts will be replaced with positive ones.

FOOD FOR THOUGHT

Write down any automatic negative thoughts you may have told yourself.

_____

_____

_____

_____

_____

_____

_____

_____

_____

_____

_____

_____

_____

II. Some Things Are Really NOT Worth the Wait

Replace each negative thought with a new positive response. Write them below. Repeat them to yourself whenever a negative thought pops into your head.

_____

_____

_____

_____

_____

_____

_____

_____

_____

_____

_____

_____

_____

III. TIME TO GET MOVING

- Perfect Wait Loss outfit: an open mind
- Schedule: 15 minutes with no distractions (location of your choice)
- Hydration: recite positive affirmations daily
- Basic Wait Loss equipment – hint – you're holding it

Any weight loss expert will tell you that the key to weight loss involves three simple things: diet, exercise, and lifestyle changes. But the hard truth is that while those three tasks may seem simple, for many people losing weight can be extremely challenging. As for me, I was never a big eater. Truthfully, on most days I ate once or maybe twice a day. I always skipped breakfast and I usually ate a late dinner and then went right to bed. Before I knew it, the pounds added up and I knew I had to do something about it.

I tried all the fad diets and magic pills and shakes, and I did get some results, but inevitably the weight would come right back. As a result, after a few unsuccessful attempts I gave up and decided to live the life of a "big girl". It wasn't a bad life for me. I was highly active, had lots of friends, dated regularly and had great jobs. Here's the thing – I knew I wasn't where I needed to be physically or emotionally. The weight was a symptom of something else.

I'll spare you the messy details but suffice it to say the weight kept me from being fully present in my life and from pursuing my dreams (or so I thought). I decided to take drastic steps and have gastric bypass surgery. Voila! The weight was no longer an issue for me. Yet, I still held off pursuing my dreams. As I began to question this dilemma within myself, I began to see understand that it wasn't my weight that was holding me back – it was my WAIT! I've learned over the years that diet, exercise and lifestyle changes are the answer to this type of Wait Loss too. Yes, it's equally challenging and a little scary but eventually I became a more centered and happier person. I'm finally working toward my purpose and not against it. I stopped WAITING and learned some lessons along the way.

> *Some days you eat salads and go to the gym. Some days you eat cupcakes and refuse to put on pants. It's called balance.*

YOU ARE WHAT YOU EAT. SO WHAT'S IN YOUR LIFE PANTRY?

We've all heard that phrase before. When applied to food it means that what we take in and digest influences our health, energy levels, mood, even behavior.

If we want to be healthy and fit then we need to eat balanced meals with fruits, vegetables, vitamins, minerals, proteins, etc. And of course, the reverse is true also. If we eat foods high in fat, salt, and sugars then we can expect those ingredients to affect our bodily organs and we may develop both physical ailments as well as a diminished mental condition. Often, we eat what's close to us, convenient and handy. So, it's vital that we keep the "good stuff" handy. We don't always get it right. The goal is to keep trying.

Interestingly, there is a pantry for your kitchen and a pantry for your life. How so? What's a life pantry? Well, a pantry as we know it is a room or storage area where we keep our food (dry goods, spices, snacks, etc.). It's usually located close to the kitchen. Think of your life pantry as added storage space for your brain. A place where additional thoughts are kept and served up when needed.

The idea here is that pantries can be stored with both healthy and unhealthy options. If your physical pantry was chock full of healthy food options you would probably include them in your dinner planning, your meals, your snacks, right? The opposite is also true. If it was stocked with the worst food choices (and we all know what they are) then chances are that's what you would wind up eating. Now let's think about the life pantry.

Fill your life pantry with healthy, positive affirmations, thoughts and people and they will nourish and feed your spirit and give you the energy you need to keep moving forward. Positivity is powerful! The

Mayo Clinic described it best stating that "positive thinking doesn't mean that you keep your head in the sand and ignore life's less pleasant situations… It simply means that you think the best is going to happen – not the worst".

Here again the reverse is true. Fill your life pantry with negative thoughts and people and you will find your energy drained.

I read a great poem recently by Lao Tzu:

Watch your thoughts, they become words. Watch your words, they become actions. Watch your actions, they become habits.

Watch your habits, they become your character. Watch your character, it becomes your destiny.

Notice how everything starts with our thoughts. What we think is either going to move us closer to or farther away from our destinies.

"As a man (or woman) thinks, so he (or she) is", Proverbs 23:7. Our thoughts, words, actions, habits and character are all shaped by what we allow ourselves to take in. We know what happens when we eat a lot of junk food. The same thing happens when we allow junk – fear, criticism, judgment, hatred, jealousy, etc. to fuel us every day.

Negativity breeds negativity. Try every day to clear your mind and your life pantry of these life draining and toxic habits and feelings. They don't work and are not good for you. So how can we fill our life pantry with positive choices?

➢ **Practice kindness** – spread good vibes and compassion to everyone around you. You will enjoy increased happiness and a healthier heart. Studies show that practicing kindness slows down the aging process and improves relationships and connections.

➢ **Focus on being positive** – Live in the moment. Forgive yourself and others for past mistakes. Practice positive affirmations.

➢ **Love and accept yourself** – Embrace you as you are. Believe that you are the perfect creation God intended you to be (even with flaws).

➢ **Laugh and smile** – Smiling from the heart and

a good belly laugh increases the production of serotonin, the happy hormone, and dopamine – these feel-good endorphins diminish feelings of stress, anxiety and depression.

➣ **Be grateful** – When we take time to notice and reflect on things, we're truly thankful for we experience more positive emotions, feel more alive, sleep better, and express more compassion. Practicing gratitude helps us to feel better and when we feel better, we are more likely to go out into the world and try to make it better.

➣ **Help someone** – "…-there is more happiness in giving than in receiving" (Acts 20:35) Give of yourself. Volunteer in the space where you are looking to make a difference. This will help you become part of that community in a much more meaningful way. It may even help you gain insight into developing the program, product, organization, etc. that you've always wanted to develop.

➣ **Be present** – Stop and take notice of the beauty and love all around you and in you. Know that you already possess everything you need to achieve your dreams.

It's important to note here that it may also be necessary to remove toxic people from your personal universe or at the very least limit your exposure to them.

Instead, maintain close relationships with people who make you feel safe, cherished and happy; people who support you and your dreams. Remember starvation diets don't work and neither does isolation.

Surround yourself with the love and light of persons who are there for you to offer hope, encouragement, laughter, a listening ear, and even a shoulder to cry on when needed. Sometimes when things aren't going exactly as we had planned, our first defense is to hide from the world. That can be very dangerous. Studies show that when we go through trying situations alone that lack of emotional support and friendship can increase our anxiety and hinder our ability to cope.

FOOD FOR THOUGHT

What toxic things can I remove from my pantry today?

_____

_____

_____

_____

_____

_____

_____

How can I bring more positivity into my life today?

_____

_____

_____

_____

_____

_____

_____

_____

Tip: Say goodbye to "friends" high in toxic ingredients. Swap out unhealthy relationships with healthier versions and enhance your journey to better living.

> **My favorite exercise used to be a cross between a lunge and a crunch.**
>
> **I called it LUNCH.**

EXERCISE! EXERCISE! EXERCISE YOUR MIND!

What makes a person give up on their dream or at the very least put it on the backburner? We've explored fear and negative feelings of self. Another dream killer is self-doubt. We begin to question whether this is something we can really do. We begin to doubt our ability to be awesome and amazing. I'm reminded of a line in the movie Sister Act 2 when Whoopi Goldberg's character was talking to Lauren Hill's character. She hands her a book and says, ""I went to my mother who gave me this book…called Letters to a Young Poet by Rainer Maria Rilke. He's a fabulous writer. A fellow used to write to him and say, 'I want to be a writer. Please read my stuff.' And Rilke says to this guy: 'Don't ask me about being a writer. If when you wake up in the morning you can think of nothing but writing…then you're a writer.'" In other words, if you write, you're a writer! If you bake, you're a baker! Get it?? There is a gift that only you possess. Cherish it. Nurture it. But use it. It's so easy to let life get in the way; to put everyone's wants and needs above our own and to convince ourselves that our idea wasn't that great in the first place. When that happens read this quote by Marianne Williamson:

> "Our deepest fear is not that we are inadequate. Our deepest fear is that we are powerful beyond measure. It is our light, not our darkness that most frightens us. We ask ourselves, 'Who am I to be brilliant, gorgeous, talented, fabulous?' Actually, who are you not to be? … And as we let our own light shine, we unconsciously give other people permission to do the same. As we are liberated from our own fear, our presence automatically liberates others."

Let's pause for another water break:

When did we learn to fear our power? What keeps us from being our true and authentic selves? Why are we so afraid? There are many experts on this topic but here's my take on it. We fear our power because deep down we know the truth. We know that if we fully embrace our inner powers, our inner gifts and strengths that we will be forced to take responsibility for our lives. We will live in and embrace the present not the past.

We will finally accept that we hold the power to alter or create the futures, careers, relationships, passions, etc. that we've always wanted. We will no longer be controlled by fear and therefore we would have no excuses.

We no longer care what naysayers think or say about us. We love and accept ourselves for who we are. We unapologetically stand in our truth and face the world with confidence. We eliminate all reasons for WAITING. And that scares us to death. It scares me too. But I push past that fear every day because I know that any time I am less than my authentic and true self – I am lost.

What about you? Do you ever feel lost? Try this: Imagine you are in a car driving to a special destination; somewhere you've always wanted to go. Along the way you make a series of wrong turns and find yourself lost. What do you do? Do you decide right then and there that you will give up on driving and never reach your destination? Do you leave your car where it is and decide you'll be better off walking home with your head hung in shame? Of course not. These options might sound ridiculous.

But that's what some of us do when we find our dreams have been detoured. Most likely you're thinking if you're lost in your car you could use a GPS, call a friend, ask a stranger for directions/help, go to the nearest gas station and ask for help, or at the very least keep driving and figure it out. Guess what? You can use these same principles in your Wait Loss journey!

➣ **Use your GPS** – God-given Positioning System – your internal navigation system or GPS is that little voice inside you that will ultimately point you towards your purpose – if you follow it. I believe God has a purpose for your life. He is prepared to help you fulfill that purpose, that goal. He's been steering you toward it all along. That's why you haven't been able to get it out of your head. It was divinely placed there just for you. Listen to it. Be guided by it. Let it direct you. Follow it.

➣ **Call a Friend** – Ask someone you trust for help or advice. Sometimes all you need is a fresh perspective, a morale boost, or a good old-fashioned heart to heart conversation about what's doable and when. Remember, a good friend isn't there to tell you what you want to hear, rather what you need to hear.

➣ **Ask a Stranger** – This one may seem a bit odd, but I bet you do it regularly. How many times have you sought out

"how-to" advice on YouTube or Pinterest?
You don't know those people, yet you
enthusiastically follow their instructions,
their recipes, their DIY hacks, etc. Lesson:
Do your research. Hear what the experts
on your subject have to say. Listen to
podcasts. Read blogs. Google it! Connect
with folks on LinkedIn. Learn from others'
examples. Reach out to them. Experts like
to share their expertise.

➢ **Go to the Nearest Gas Station** – Fill
up on all the knowledge you can and
become an expert on your dream. Check
out books from your local library.

➢ **Keep Driving and Figure it Out** – Don't
give up. Don't stop and walk away from
your dream. Find another route if necessary.
Backtrack and see where things went wrong
and regroup. Have faith in yourself and your
ability to make it work. You can do it!

FOOD FOR THOUGHT

Where is my GPS directing me?

_____

_____

_____

_____

_____

_____

_____

Name one person that will support you in your Wait Loss journey. Call them today and talk to them about this new adventure. Ask for their honest advice.

_____

_____

_____

_____

_____

_____

_____

III. Time to Get Moving

Where can I find information on my dream? List two sources. Look them up today. Write down what you learn.

_____

_____

_____

_____

_____

_____

_____

_____

> **Diet Day 1: I have removed all the bad food from the house. It was delicious!**

STOP STARVING YOUR DREAMS

For anyone who's ever struggled with typical weight loss (as I have) we know that most diets don't work. As dieters we start out very well intentioned and motivated but oftentimes our focus is on the foods we can't have. Again – we focus on the negative aspects of the diet. Right off the bat we're discouraged. How is that helpful? Then, as soon as we stop dieting, we begin not only to crave but eventually indulge in all those foods we tried so hard to avoid.

We go back to our poor eating habits and well... the rest is history. This same scenario is true for Wait Loss. We start out so pumped up and ready to go but somewhere along the line we begin to focus on the negatives. We replay all those old messages that tell us we can't do it, that we won't be successful, and that it doesn't matter. Just where do those messages originate? Maybe it was a teacher or parent or another adult who asked the dreaded question, "What do you want to be when you grow up?" That's a loaded question to be sure. A child may respond with any myriad of answers; ballerina, astronaut, superhero, etc. only to be shot down with comments like (real world, grown up, support family, etc., etc.) And thus, begins a life of stifling the creative voice inside of us.

Blogger, Emily Jordan, got it so right. She said:

"What if we changed our mindset from trying to make ourselves fit into a job, to trying to make a job that fit ourselves? We must understand that each of our purposes and paths to fulfillment are unique, and we have to trust that we will get there when we are brave enough to honor who we are. We cannot keep reinforcing the belief that all of us will succeed and be happy in a traditional career path, because it makes those of us who don't find fulfillment there feel like failures, like we've done something wrong. *Instead, we need to promote the truth — to children and adults alike — that the path to fulfillment is simply to be true to who you are and use your uniqueness to serve the world in some way.*"

Here are some suggestions to help you change your lifestyle and lose your WAIT.

1. **Be an original.** Avoid trends and fads and the tendency to jump on the current bandwagon. Remember you are unique. You don't have to do, be, act, or look like anyone else to find success or happiness. Be determined to share your gift with the world in a way that only you can. The world needs you. And don't forget that while there may be nothing new under the sun as someone once said. I assure you there may very well be a new way to approach it, tackle it, fix it, and change it – for the better.

2. **Don't be afraid to fail.** There are countless examples of extremely successful people who failed repeatedly. Here are a few:

   a. **J. K. Rowling** – (Author Harry Potter series) – ""I had failed on an epic scale. An exceptionally short-lived marriage had imploded, and I was jobless, a lone parent, and as poor as it is possible to be in modern Britain, without being homeless. The fears that my parents had had for me, and that I had had for myself, had both come to pass, and by every usual standard, I was the biggest failure I knew." Coming out of this failure stronger and more determined was the key to her success. This woman never gave up. Think about her story for a minute.

J.K. Rowling had just gotten a divorce, was on government aid (welfare!), and could barely afford to feed her baby in 1994. This was three years before the first Harry Potter book, *Harry Potter and The Philosopher's Stone*, was published. When she was shopping it around, she was so poor she couldn't afford a computer or even the cost of photocopying the 90,000-word novel, so she **manually** typed out each version to send to publishers. Can you imagine having to type multiple copies of a 90,000-word novel – only to have it rejected again and again? It was rejected dozens of times until finally Bloomsbury, a small London publisher, gave it a second chance after the CEO's eight-year-old daughter fell in love with it.

This formerly rejected author didn't let failure define her; rather it inspired her to keep going. That's exactly what she did and look at where she is today. Rowling's books have been translated into over 80 languages, won multiple awards, and sold more than 500 copies worldwide, becoming the best-selling book series in history. That first book, Harry Potter and the Philosopher's Stone, received immediate popular and critical accolades. What followed were six further best-selling books and eight blockbuster films. The former penniless Rowling is now worth at least $670 million with some estimates putting her net worth at $1.2 billion thanks to her Harry Potter franchise of books, movies, theme parks, paraphernalia and more.

b. **Vera Wang** (fashion and jewelry designer) – Did you know that Vera didn't start out wanting to be in the fashion business? Hard to believe but it's true. Today, Wang is a fashion icon and undeniably one of the world's most famous designers. That was not her original dream. Wang had high hopes of becoming a professional figure skater. Her disappointment came in 1986 when she didn't make the U.S. Olympics team. Dejected she took a retail job at a Yves Saint Laurent boutique in New York City and two years later found herself at Vogue. She started out as an assistant and worked her way up the ladder to become one of Vogue magazine's youngest ever fashion editors; a journey that would take 15 years. But how did she get into designing wedding dresses? As she was planning her wedding to Arthur Becker, she came to the realization that something was missing in the bridal industry. She thought the then present wedding gown designs did nothing for the needs of the modern bride.

So, she started designing her own brand of wedding gowns. Today, Wang is reportedly worth an estimated $650 million. Get this, she earns her money through wedding gown sales as well as figure skating gowns that she has created. Talk about coming full circle! Lesson: Failure led Wang to find her "finally" moment.

What's a finally moment you ask? It's the moment you finally figure out who you are. It's the moment you finally begin to recognize and embrace what makes you special. It's the moment you're finally ready to let go of the baggage that's been weighing you down for what seems and feels like forever. It's the moment you finally show up for you. This moment looks and feels different for each of us. It may show up when it's time to let go of a toxic relationship, job, spouse, or even a painful memory. Only you will know when you have reached your finally moment. You'll know it because it will give you your long-awaited permission to breathe, to live, to love and to just be. What's your finally moment? Maybe it's happening right now as you're reading this book. Maybe it will come when you finally give yourself permission to be the YOU you've always wanted to be. Only you will know when that marvelous and majestic time has arrived.

But trust me, when it does your heart will soar!

3. **Retrain your brain.** Maybe it's time to rethink what makes you happy; really happy. Happiness does not come from a title, or paycheck or adoration and accolades. Happiness does not come from the way you look in a mirror, how much you weigh, or what you eat. True happiness comes when we align ourselves with our purpose, our unique calling in life. Happiness comes from pursuing our dreams. I believe our dreams are God's way of whispering in our ears and gently steering us toward our reason for being. The tiny seeds of these dreams

were planted in us long ago, in our hearts and minds and it's up to us to develop them and make them grow. But over time we trample those buds and wonder why our souls are not growing. We wonder why we don't feel right.

We know that something is out of whack, but we can't seem to put our fingers on it. The farther away we are from what makes us truly unique, the more we feel ill at ease. Dis-ease comes from the dis-comfort we feel when our actions are not aligned with our true purpose. We all know the benefits of alignment (spines, tires, etc.). Here's a new way to think about it. After losing his mother to breast cancer, biologist Stephen Le set out on a journey to see if there was anything he could do to reduce the risk of cancer which ran in his family. His search took him from Canada to China, Kenya, Australia, India, North America and finally to his ancestral home Vietnam. He returned home with an interesting theory: our meals should align with what our ancestors ate, not with the latest fad. He even wrote a book about it:

III. Time to Get Moving

100 Million Years of Food: What Our Ancestors Ate and Why It Matters. To put it simply his argument is that we are predisposed to best process/digest the same diets our families ate 500 years ago. According to Le, the farther we stray away from our ancestral diets the more we rely on mass-produced food often loaded with chemicals that contribute to – you guessed it! – diseases, such as cancer, heart disease, and obesity. So, here's my very unscientific hypothesis. If our bodies are pre-disposed to certain foods which once digested can improve our physical health and well- being then our hearts our mind and our spirit can likewise be pre-disposed to a singular purpose which once realized and actuated can be the best line of defense in protecting our mental health and well-being which will lead to us feeling great. Now do you get it? We really can feel better. We can feel great. **We can be happy – but only if we choose to be happy.**

Food for Thought

Finish this sentence. I am my happiest when…

_____

_____

_____

_____

_____

_____

_____

_____

_____

_____

What would my world look like if I started doing more of the things that made me happy?

_____

_____

_____

_____

_____

III. Time to Get Moving

What can I do today to start having more of those happy moments in my life?

_____

_____

_____

_____

_____

_____

_____

IV. CHOOSE HAPPINESS

> "Happiness is a choice, not a result. Nothing will you happy until you CHOOSE to be happy."
>
> - Ralph Marston

WHEN WAS THE LAST TIME you felt truly happy? Somewhere along the line we started linking how we may be feeling at a certain time to who we are as individuals. We think – I'm unhappy because I am (fill in the blank). For some, the word or words in the blank space is alone, not good enough, unmarried, overweight, etc. etc. Here's a quick lesson to help you rethink that position. Right now, as I'm writing this, I'm hungry.

I skipped dinner and now my stomach is growling.

I am hungry. It doesn't mean that I'm a greedy person. It doesn't mean that I have an eating disorder. I'll grab a quick bite soon, feel better and get back to work. Reasonable right? The key to retraining your brain is to apply new thought processes to old thoughts. Remember, FEELINGS are temporary; they refer to what we may be experiencing at any given time. BEING refers to our existence, who we are, specific traits that brand us.

Instead of saying this:	Say this:	Do this:
I'm alone	I'm feeling lonely right now.	Reach out to a friend
I'm insecure	I'm feeling insecure	Ask for advice
I'm unhappy because I work at a job that I hate	My job does not give me a sense of fulfillment	Search for and embrace your true passion

Does any of this sound too simplistic? Is happiness really a choice? Can you really retrain your brain? I know you can. It all starts with believing that the happiness you seek dwells within you. What if I told you that years ago someone planted ten million dollars in your back yard? What would you do? Would you say I'll get to it one day? Would you WAIT for the kids to grow up, or for your pressures at work to ease up, or for retirement? OR would you run out to the nearest home improvement store and buy shovels, lights, pickaxes, tents and anything else you thought you might need?

Would you find time, make time, steal time from other nonessential activities to get your dig on??? Of course, you would! And you wouldn't stop until you found the buried treasure. Here's what I want you know and believe. Buried deep inside you is a treasure that would rival the Pharaohs of ancient Egypt! Buried deep within you is the answer you've been looking for; the key to your happiness; the path to your purpose. What are you waiting for? It's time to start digging!

How are you feeling right now? Let's take another water break:

A common thread among serial procrastinators like us is that sometimes we just don't know where and how to start. We know we need to do something, but the task seems so large, so daunting that putting it off somehow makes more sense. We WAIT until we think we have it all figured out. Here's the thing – when does anybody ever have it all figured out? Never! I have a tool that just might help you get started.

It's called Ikigai (ik-ki-guy). Ikigai is a Japanese concept that means "a reason for being". Loosely translated the word refers to having a direction or purpose in life; something that makes life worthwhile. I like to think of it as the reason your heart beats; the thing that gets you up in the morning. There are books, workshops, papers, and videos that you can devour on this topic. What I'm going to share with you is a simplified version. I call it Ikigai Lite. Please do yourself a favor and read up on Ikigai. Good stuff!

To begin your Ikigai journey, first understand that the concept overlaps four key areas of your life.

Answer these four questions:

1. **What do you love? (What are you passionate about?)**

   How to answer. Consider what you would do if money was no object. What do you enjoy talking about? If you could spend some spare time doing whatever you wanted to do – what would it be? What would you do if you didn't have to worry about making money?

2. **What are you good at? (What is your vocation?)**

   How to answer: Consider your unique natural abilities, your talents, and skills. What are those talents that come easy to you? What is that thing that you can do "in your sleep"?

3. **What does the world need? (What is your mission?)**

   How to answer: Consider what you can give to the world, your culture or your family. What societal problems would you like to address and/or help solve immediately? What community issue touches you emotionally?

4. **What can you get paid for? (What is your profession?)**

   How to answer: Consider activities that can provide financial compensation (after all you still must take care of yourself and your family – and eat.) Are you already getting paid to do what you want to do, what you love to do? If you could get paid to do what you love – what would that be?

Some people use Venn diagrams to answer the above questions (see below). Here is what I am suggesting. Take some time to think about the questions and write down whatever words pop into your mind. Do not worry about spelling or order or even meaning. Just write. When you are finished look for areas of natural overlap and then look to see if there are any places where they intersect. The goal is to have all the intersecting parts in balance. Your center (chart center) is the key to your personal ikigai. Give it a try. The results may surprise you.

Ikigai Diagram

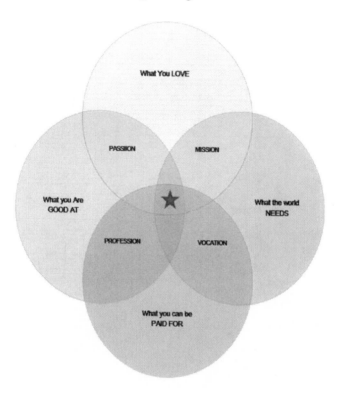

Use the next page to write your answers to the questions from page 70-71

FOOD FOR THOUGHT

What makes you truly happy?

_____

_____

_____

_____

What are you good at?

_____

_____

_____

_____

_____

What does the world need?

_____

_____

_____

_____

_____

IV. Choose Happiness

What can you get paid to do?

_____

_____

_____

_____

_____

_____

V. CALIBRATE YOUR INNER SCALE

I put my scale in the corner of the bathroom today and that's where it'll stay until it apologizes.

A CONVERSATION ABOUT WAIT LOSS would be incomplete about a few words on how to balance the scales. In the world of physical weight loss, the scale is an important tool for keeping track of progress or lack thereof. But it can be discouraging. It can be a hindrance to success. The same is true in Wait Loss. If we're not careful we can become slaves to our inner scale, and it will become yet another distraction in the pursuit of our purpose. How so?

Think about how you may have felt standing on a

physical scale. If you're anything like me, you instantly begin to make judgments about yourself. "I'm too big." "I'm too small." I only lost 1 pound – I'm a failure." I might have been pleased with the progress I was making to date only to throw those good feelings out of the window based on the number on that scale. I tied the number on the scale to not only by body image but my image of me. We can be guilty of the same sabotage when it comes to our Wait Loss. Mental changes are not always as easy to detect as physical changes. As a result, the numbers on our inner scale can be deceptive.

What's an inner scale? It's the mental tool we use to measure ourselves against ourselves. We ask: how am I doing? Am I doing it right? Am I making enough progress? Am I on the right track? Should I do more? Is this enough? Am I enough? And on and on and on. The answers we tell ourselves either motivate us forward or hold us back. What I want you to remember is that starting any new program is usually the hardest part. Don't let antiquated measuring techniques (aka automated negative thoughts) control you, derail you.

Being controlled by your inner scale can make it harder to keep going especially if you don't immediately see the anticipated changes. Remember, when trying to lose physical weight, most of us need weeks and weeks of proper diet and exercise before we see any real change to the scale. And even then, those numbers might go up and down based on all kinds of factors, i.e., time of day, time of the month, etc. The same is true for Wait Loss. Making significant life changes will take patience, hard work, and time. The goal is a happier life not instant gratification.

How can you avoid being a slave to your scale? Here are a few tips:

1. **Have regularly scheduled self-check-ins.**
   Don't feel obligated to check in with yourself every minute of every day. Don't drive yourself (and everyone around you) crazy with unreasonable expectations. Try setting weekly and monthly goals. Review what you wrote down in the "Food for Thought" section. Pick one activity to focus on and once that one is mastered move on to the next one.

2. If tip number one feels too heavy, **consider eliminating your inner scale all together and focus instead on how you feel**. Trust yourself to know that you are on the right path.

3. Remember, **Wait Loss will not come without consistency and determination**. Focus on learning the techniques shared in this book.

   Get to know and understand what will work best for you. Work on building the strength and endurance you will need to see this journey through to its glorious end.

READY, SET, GO!

Before starting a typical weight loss program, experts will tell you that several factors can have a significant impact on your level of success. Perhaps it's making changes to your diet, exercise, and lifestyle. It could be using tools and tips that keep you on track. Knowing what not to do is always helpful, as is getting help from those with some insight on the topic. They may tell you that in the end only a customized program designed just for you will work. These are all excellent suggestions. Hopefully, this book will get you started in the right direction as you begin your Wait Loss program. Let's recap:

a. **Stock your life pantry with wholesome foods:** Feed your mind, heart, body, and spirit with positive energy and vibes. Surround yourself with people who will love and support you through this journey. Fill your life pantry with healthy, wholesome, choices that will give you the motivation you need to turn your dreams into reality. Get rid of toxic distractions.

b. **Exercise your mind:** Discover that thing that gets you up in the morning. Learn everything you can about your purpose in life. Talk to trusted advisors. Seek out experts. Do your due diligence and read up on what has worked in the past, what hasn't worked and what's missing. Strive to provide that missing link.

c. **Feed your dreams:** Don't let tired and old life lessons keep you from pursuing your heart's desire. It's not too late to be the person you wanted to be when you grew up. Trust yourself and your gift. Don't be afraid to fail. Redefine your goals. Pursue what makes you happy. Find your Ikigai.

Remember, only you can decide when the time is right for you; only you can set your feet to the path prepared for you. The happiness you seek is within you. Here's to the beginning of your journey. Enjoy!

I'd love to hear from you. If you want to share your Wait Loss success, stories, strategies, etc. feel free to email me at stacijscott@gmail.com.

Last water break:

I told you I love quotes. Here are some great ones to help you lose your WAIT:

> "If you wait until you are ready, you'll be waiting for the rest of your life". – Alicia Dunams (international model turned entrepreneur and author)

> "Change will not come if we WAIT for some other person or some other time. We are the ones we've been waiting for. We are the change that we seek." – President Barack Obama

> "Do not WAIT; the time will never be 'just right'. Start where you stand, and work with whatever tools you may have at your command, and better tools will be found as you go along." George Herbert (poet)

> "Learn to enjoy every minute of your life.

Be happy now. Don't WAIT for something outside of yourself to make you happy in the future. Think how precious your time is, whether it's at work or with your family. Every minute should be enjoyed and savored." – Earl Nightingale (speaker, radio host)

➤ "Infuse your life with action. Don't WAIT for it to happen. Make it happen. Make your own love. And whatever your beliefs, honor your creator, not by passively waiting for grace to come down from upon high, but by doing what you can to make grace happen…yourself, right now, right down here on Earth." – Bradley Whitford (actor)

➤ Living in the moment means letting go of the past and not waiting for the future. It means living your life consciously, aware that each moment you breathe is a gift. – Oprah Winfrey

➤ "Don't be afraid to engage all of your senses and take in everything that life has to offer. SEE yourself winning and pursuing your goal. HEAR the voice inside you pushing you toward your greatness. Take the leap and TOUCH someone's life today (even if it's yours). TASTE and see how amazing life is when you are aligned with your purpose. Do it today. Lose the wait and FEEL great!"
– **Staci Scott** ☺

AFTERWORD

I am no longer waiting for a special occasion; I burn the best candles on ordinary days.

I am no longer waiting for the house to be clean; I fill it with people who understand that even dust is Sacred.

I am no longer waiting for everyone to understand me; It's just not their task

I am no longer waiting for the perfect children; my children have their own names that burn as brightly as any star.

I am no longer waiting for the other shoe to drop; It already did, and I survived.

I am no longer waiting for the time to be right; the time is always now.

I am no longer waiting for the mate who will complete me; I am grateful to be so warmly, tenderly held.

Afterword

I am no longer waiting for a quiet moment; my heart can be stilled whenever it is called.

I am no longer waiting for the world to be at peace; I unclench my grasp and breathe peace in and out.

I am no longer waiting to do something great; being awake to carry my grain of sand is enough.

I am no longer waiting to be recognized; I know that I dance in a holy circle.

I am no longer waiting for Forgiveness. I believe, I Believe.

-Mary Anne Perrone

Amen Sister Mary!!

Dear Reader,

As I sit writing this message I cannot fully express how humble, grateful, and appreciative I am that you are holding my book in your hands.

For me, completing my first book is not the culmination of my wait loss journey but rather the first of many steps. Just as physical weight loss requires commitment, dedication, and patience, our mental wait loss will take hard work, determination and tenacity.

I wholeheartedly believe that we can do this. Hopefully, I've given you a gentle nudge in the right direction. Yes, we still have our hectic lives and busy schedules. We still have to care for so many responsibilities.
Just remember to put your oxygen mask on first. Take care of you. Take care of your heart. Make yourself a priority. You are worth it. I believe in you. Thank you so much for your support.

Staci

REFERENCES

Jordan, Emily (2017 Nov 28). *Stop Asking People What They Want To Be When They Grow Up*. Retrieved from: https://medium.com/thrive-global/stop-asking-people-what-they-want-to-be-when-they-grow-up-385669c1251f

Stress Management (2020 March 21). Retrieved from https://www.mayoclinic.org/healthy-lifestyle/stress-management/basics/stress-relief/hlv-20049495

ABOUT THE AUTHOR

To say that I've given much thought about what to include in this particular section is a huge understatement. Ultimately, I did what most new authors do. I spent time reading blogs, reviewing what the experts said must be included, and even had a robust conversation with my writing coach and book doula Geo Derice. In the end I decided that far more important than my credentials and accomplishments is this message.

There is no one magic answer when it comes to living the life you've imagined for yourself. There....I said it. So why did I write a book about it and why should you read it? Just like so many people, and maybe you too, I've struggled with making my self, my health, my dreams, even my life a priority. I know what it means and what it feels like to take care of everything and everyone else first leaving little or worse zero time to focus on what makes my heart happy. What I learned along my journey is that clarity of vision and purpose does not eliminate all of the things that pull on my time on any given day.

I am still a mother, sister, aunt, employee, employer, friend, mentor, entrepreneur, author, speaker, coach, counselor, board member, student, teacher, homeowner, radio host, dieter, etc., etc. Here's what I know for sure. It is only when I am working on being the best version of myself for myself that I can successfully and sanely manage all of the roles and responsibilities that make up my life. This book started out as a personal letter to me, a way to stay motivated as I began my wait loss journey. There were lessons along the way, highs and lows, successes and disappointments. Some days I get it incredibly right and some days I don't. But then I pick up this book and get back on track.

I'm hoping that by sharing what I've learned, you

too can jumpstart your wait loss journey. We really are in this together.

Remember to have an amazingly adventurous life. What are you waiting for??

Take care,

Staci

Fun Facts About Staci:

1. Love 80s old school hip hop (favorite rapper Rakim)

2. Chocolate!

3. Playing Scattergories

4. Historical African American romance novels, favorite author Beverly Jenkins.

CONTACT INFO

I'd love to keep in touch with you and hear your wait loss stories.

Email:

stacijscott@gmail.com

Find me on LinkedIn at:

https://www.linkedin.com/in/staci-scott-mhs-6706095

(For Bulk Book Orders Use The Email Above To Get Discounted Pricing)

Made in the USA
Middletown, DE
06 November 2021

51788558R00061